GET OUT OF THAT BED!

A devotional guide through the book of John

C.L. "SHEP" Shepherd

SHEP INSPIRES LLC

CONTENTS

INTRODUCTION

It was a day I would never forget, over 16 years ago now. My mentor Sid and I sat parked in a green Ford Expedition, outside of a high school on the Southside of Atlanta, Georgia. We had just finished speaking to our second group of kids at an FCA meeting and were preparing to head over to our final school for the day. I began looking through my notes, hoping to ensure I was prepared for the next sermon I was to share with this final group. Public speaking is my greatest fear, so preparation is one of the tools I use to calm the nerves as much as possible. I felt fairly confident that the first two talks went well, and was excited to share my next talk with the team I would be in front of in about an hour. Subtly, with a calm polite tone, looking straight ahead through the front windshield, Sid asked, "Shep, what are you doing?" Without missing a beat I replied, "getting ready to knock it out the park again, hopefully." This time he turned toward me, fixed his gaze and asked again, "Shep why aren't you sharing your story with these groups?" The question caught me off guard. "There is nothing special about me or my story," I thought. All I wanted to do was tell kids about how much God loved them, and how He had an awesome plan for their lives. "Brother, nobody wants to hear about my sad and boring background" I replied. After a long quiet pause, Sid tapped my knee gently with his right hand. As soon as his hand connected, he said it. With the same calm loving tone as earlier, but infused with supernatural authority this time, Sid said, Shep share your story."

It took courage, transparency, and vulnerability that I had never really tapped in to prior-- but that afternoon I began sharing my story. Sharing the story of what God had done in and around my life since He rescued me from a suicide attempt at 14 years old. After sharing at evangelistic events globally and seeing hundreds of thousands of lives transformed by the Gospel for nearly two decades, I am so grateful God spoke to me through my buddy Sid! My story has taken me around the world and thankfully has now brought you and I together.

The most common question I get from new followers of Jesus involves where to begin in their journey of reading God's Word. My reply consistently has been the same: "Start with John." I encourage people to start with John because of the powerful sense of urgency he conveys, and how every record he took regarding the life of Christ just jumps off the pages. This guide is simply 55 reflections to help assist you as you walk through the book of John and begin (or rekindle) your journey in following Christ. I challenge and encourage you to get out of your bed daily, and make spending time in prayer and God's word a priority. My prayer is that this devotional will bless you and make you a blessing, in Jesus' name--Amen.

THE WORD

Read: John 1:1-3

◆ ◆ ◆

Let's start this journey right. As a matter of fact, let's commit to starting every day for the rest of the days we have breath left in our bodies right. If we are going to start them right, they must begin with THE WORD. What a perfect example of this we find in the opening chapter of John: "In the beginning was the Word…" (John 1:1). Jesus Christ, the greatest man to ever live, left us a love letter called the bible, and He desires for us to read, reflect, study, and meditate on it daily. This is essential for our growth and maturity as followers of Jesus. We can't go around, over, or under it… If we want to know Jesus, we must fully immerse ourselves in His word…DAILY!

THE LIGHT

Read: John 1:4-18

◆ ◆ ◆

From the very start of this passage, we begin to learn about the life that is found in Jesus. This is also where we discover that the life in Jesus is the "...light of men" (John 1:4). We then begin to learn very specific truths about this light, and also about John's purpose. We read that "There was a man named John who was sent from God. He came as a witness to testify about the light, so that all might believe..." (John 1:6-7). You and I have that same light shining in and through us now. We also have a very similar responsibility to testify about the love, life, and light of Jesus Christ. Jesus gives this light to all who believe. In verse 12 it literally says, "But to all who did receive Him, He gave the right to be children of God..." (John 1:12). What that means is we don't **have to** be a light, we **get to** be a light. It is a privilege, an honor, and a major blessing for us as believers in Jesus Christ to be called His children, and be given an opportunity to shine bright for Him. It is important that I take this opportunity to point out one more detail from earlier in verse 5. This verse tells us that the life in Christ, which we have learned is the light, "...shines in the darkness, yet the darkness did not overcome it" (John 1:5). If our light shines most brightly in the dark places of our world, it is imperative that we let our light shine in those places and for those people. We have to boldly and fearlessly allow His light to shine through us. The darkness cannot overcome God's light, but God's light can and will overcome the darkness, if you and I commit to letting His light shine...DAILY!

- Privilege to live a child of God
- As believers in Jesus: birth, death, and resurrection.
- Christ is Light
- Christ has seen God
- Christ is God

HIS GLORY

Read: John 1:19-28

❖ ❖ ❖

As you allow the light of Christ to shine through you daily, remember that it is not about you. It is and always will be about Jesus. In verse 19 we begin to see that when you are living out your purpose and allowing Christ to shine through you, people are going to start asking questions. Our job is to make sure we always give the glory to God and always point people back to Him. Maybe you have a particular gift, skill, resources, career, or ability that bring you a significant amount of notoriety; that is great and I applaud you. As a follower of Jesus now, you have the awesome opportunity to use that influence to point even more people to your Savior, Jesus Christ. John says it this way, "…I am a voice of one crying out in the wilderness: Make straight the way of the Lord just as Isaiah the prophet said" (John 1:23). Not only does he point people to the greatness of Jesus, John also finds time to give honor to someone who came before him, the prophet Isaiah. What a tremendous example for us to model as well—to use all that we are to honor those who played a part in shaping who we've become. Most importantly, let us use our influence great and small to proclaim the magnificence of Jesus. When you are driving down the street and see a stop, one way, right turn, or yield sign—you don't get out of your vehicle, bow down and worship the sign do you? Of course not! In that same manner, we shouldn't allow people to worship us or the awesomeness of our ability…instead, people should see

4

our lives and it lead them directionally to a closer relationship with Jesus Christ. Always remember, we are just signs on the road of life pointing people towards Jesus...DAILY!

- We are signs on the road pointing others to Jesus

- John baptizing Jews was to question since only Gentiles were baptized into the Jewish faith

2:1 - John was saying he was not worthy to be Jesus Slave

COME AND SEE

Read: John 1:29-51

◆ ◆ ◆

When we meet Jesus and truly begin to follow Him, the natural progression is to tell somebody else. In verse 29 John sees Jesus, then in verse 36 John tells two of his disciples. In verse 38 John's disciples meet Jesus, and in verse 41 Andrew (one the two disciples) goes to tell his brother Simon. Then in verse 42 he brings Simon to Jesus. In verse 43 Jesus finds Philip, and in verse 45 Philip tells Nathanael about Jesus. In verse 46 Philip then invites Nathanael to come and see Jesus for himself. Nathanael was expressing some apprehension, but came anyway. We have met Jesus and have been filled with His light, so we must tell someone also. Our relationship with Jesus is personal but it is not private! Whether it is our friends, family, teammates, coworkers, or even a stranger, we must be intentional regarding telling others about Jesus…DAILY!

DISCIPLES BELIEVED

Read: John 2:1-12

◆ ◆ ◆

Chapter 2 begins with the first recorded miracle that Jesus performed. Jesus attends a wedding with His family and disciples, and ends up turning six jars of water into wine. Wow! An amazing miracle that to this day, I must admit, my mind cannot fully comprehend. But my heart does believe it. Speaking of believing, there is one specific verse I want to highlight. Toward the end of this passage, we discover that "Jesus performed this first sign in Cana of Galilee. He displayed His glory, and His disciples believed in Him" (John 2:11). Wait, what?! You mean you can be a disciple and still have growing to do as a believer? Yes. The more you walk with Jesus, the more you and I get to witness displays of His glory, and with every display we will grow in faith and belief. Be patient with yourself as you continue to walk more and more closely with our great and mighty God... DAILY!

THE TEMPLE

Read: John 2:13-25

◆ ◆ ◆

In these particular verses we see how passionate Jesus is about His Father's house, and also how important doing the right thing within the temple is to Him. Interestingly, in verse 19 Jesus uses the term *sanctuary* as an illustration for His body. If protecting the temple is important to Jesus, it should be important to us as well. We must make it a priority to be very intentional about what goes into our bodies, and be just as passionate about the things that we need to keep out of our bodies. As a follower of Jesus Christ we must eat and hydrate properly, we also must exercise and ensure we are getting proper rest. Our bodies are the only place on earth where we truly live, so we must take care of our *sanctuary*...DAILY!

FRESH START

Read: John 3:1-21

◆ ◆ ◆

Whether it is a hot cup of coffee, a brisk run or walk, a hot shower, a delicious breakfast, a time of prayer, or a devotion… nothing beats a fresh start to your day. Starting your morning the right way often sets the pace for the state of mind and spirit you will be in for the rest of day, so they are critical for optimum performance. As we encounter this passage, we witness a discussion between Jesus and a man named Nicodemus, who has come to Jesus at night with some questions. Jesus' first words to him are: "…I assure you: Unless someone is born again, he cannot see the Kingdom of God" (John 3:3). Jesus is telling this man that not only is a fresh start a good thing for our day, apparently a *fresh start* is necessary for us to spend eternity with God. We must be born again—meaning we must confess and repent of our sin, acknowledge Christ as our Savior and Lord, and be baptized. Good people don't go to heaven, forgiven people do! Forgiveness is only available through Jesus Christ because of the finished work on the cross. Any of us who are planning on spending eternity with Christ must be born again. May we demonstrate our gratitude for the fresh start that has been given to us through Jesus… DAILY!

REAL LOVE

Read: John 3:16

◆ ◆ ◆

This verse is probably the most well known in all of the bible, and
for good reason. It speaks of the amazing love that God has for us,
by sending His one and only Son Jesus into the world to save all
those who believe. The thing I love most about verse 16 is that it
is one of the verses in the bible that you and I can place our names
into, and it will still be biblically accurate. I'm serious! Try it...
insert your name below in the blanks and then read it aloud...

"For God loved ___the World___ *in this way: He gave*
His One and Only Son, so that if ___whoever___
believes in Him, _____ *will not perish, but*
_____ *[will] have eternal life."* (John 3:16)

This truth changed my life, and it will change yours. Allow
this truth to seep into your heart, allow it to take root
in your mind, allow it to wash over you... DAILY!

THE ONE

Read: John 3:22-36

◆ ◆ ◆

Every good thing in and around our lives would not be possible if it wasn't for God. The problem is, we often think because God has given us so much, *that's* why He exists. Truth is, God doesn't exist for our pleasure—we exist for His. Everything you have, everything you are, everything you have potential to be is ultimately purposed to give Glory back to God. John communicates this most effectively when he says, "He must increase, but I must decrease. The One who comes from above is above all…" (John 3:30-31). As followers of Jesus, He is first. Everyone and everything else is a distant second. We must make it a priority to keep Jesus on the throne of our lives in word and in deed. Let us intentionally live a surrendered lifestyle that demonstrates the supremacy of God…DAILY!

GREATER

Read: John 4:1-26

◆ ◆ ◆

As we begin chapter 4 we read of how Jesus leaves Judea while heading towards Galilee, passes thru Samaria, and has this intriguing exchange with a Samaritan woman. This woman had clearly heard of Jesus, but interestingly did not recognize Him when she saw and was speaking to Him. Let's put a coin in the meter and park there for a moment... This can be true of many of us. So many times God is speaking to us, but we miss it because we haven't invested adequate time into deeply knowing Him, and developing a keen ear for His voice. My prayer is that we make the leap from the outskirts of relationship, and dive deeply into closely walking with Jesus. Okay, in verse 7 Jesus asks the woman to give Him a drink of water...then in verse 10 He begins to tell her about the living water that He gives. Jesus then explains this incredible truth saying, "everyone who drinks from this water will get thirsty again. But whoever drinks from the water I will give him will never thirst again- ever! In fact, the water I will give him will become a well of water springing up within him for eternal life" (John 4:13-14). Whatever God is instructing us to give Him, is minor compared to what He has to offer us in return. Some of the expectations that come with this new life in Christ may seem a little overwhelming, and sometimes we wonder, can we really do this? The good news is, first of all, we aren't alone. Second of all, whatever God is instructing us to give Him is so that He can give us something much greater in return. So don't focus on the task, focus on the greater outcome of being obedient...DAILY!

REAL DEAL

Read: John 4:27-42

◆ ◆ ◆

As we continue to journey through this chapter, we see again how someone meets Jesus and can't help but run and tell someone. This woman leaves everything she has and goes into town to tell the men what happened to her, and that they should come see for themselves. Intrigued by her story, these people come and spend two days listening to Jesus. Then something powerful happens. They look at the Samaritan woman and say, "we no longer believe because of what you said, for we have heard for ourselves and know that this really is the Savior of the world" (John 4:42). What an incredible example of true growth and spiritual maturity! Yes, it is awesome that someone may be open to learning more about Jesus because of what we have said or done—but the ultimate goal is to see them come to know Jesus for themselves, and begin to walk in relationship with Him. Be an example, be a voice, share your story, but most importantly, get out of the way so people can see that Jesus is the real deal for themselves...DAILY!

ONE WORD

Read: John 4:43-54

◆ ◆ ◆

During this passage Jesus finally makes it to Galilee, and is immediately met by a royal official with an urgent request. What happens next is another powerful miracle, and sign that Jesus is who He said He is. This man begs Jesus to come heal his sick son before he dies. Jesus responds, "Go... your son will live. The man believed what Jesus said to him and departed" (John 4:50). Before the man even makes it back home he is met with the good news that his son was healed. Jesus healed this man's son, and unlike the water He turned into wine, He wasn't even in the same room with him. Think about it—Jesus said one word and a miracle happened. Many of us have things in our lives that we know are dying and won't survive unless God turns it around. We must do as this official did and boldly take our request to God. Also like this official, we must be obedient to what God says and *believe* what He says—despite what we see. Even though it may appear that Jesus is far away from the thing you need Him to heal, trust and believe that one word from Him can change everything. So whatever things you posses that need life to be restored in them, take them to Jesus... DAILY!

Don't make excuse. + just do it!"

GET UP

Read: John 5:1-15

◆ ◆ ◆

Chapter 5 begins with yet another miracle, as we read about one of the men lying by the pool of Bethesda, who has been sick for 38 years. Jesus asks the man if he wants to get well, and he immediately delves into his list of excuses for why he can't. He had a story he had told himself for so long that it limited him from seeing the opportunity in front of him. He felt defeated because he had no one to help him into the pool, and it always seemed like everyone else was getting ahead instead of him. Many of us have our own narrative that we have been playing over and over in our minds as well, and just like this man lying by the pool, sick for 38 years, our excuses and defeated dialogue have gotten us nowhere. Jesus paid no attention to this man's negative thinking or limitations. He didn't say, "I'll go get some guys to help you"—Jesus told him to "get up... pick up your mat and walk" (John 5:8). We also must stop making excuses, and realize God can strengthen us to do for ourselves what we have been waiting on others to do for us. Refuse to accept a life of lame living. Get up, pick up what you need, and walk...DAILY!

ALIVE

Read: John 5:16-47

◆ ◆ ◆

Throughout this passage of scripture, Jesus further explains the dynamic between God the Father and God the Son. We begin to understand their oneness, and the authority given to Jesus on earth. Jesus illuminates this when He says, "I assure you: Anyone who hears My word and believes Him who sent Me has eternal life and will not come under judgement but has passed from death to life" (John 5:24). Until we hear God's word and believe in Him, we are all dead in our sin. We may be able to walk, talk, watch tv, play a sport, or go shopping...but spiritually we are dead men or women walking. We haven't lived until we have the life and light of Christ to awaken our souls and give our lives true meaning and purpose. That life comes only to those who truly and fully believe Jesus is who He says He is, and He can do what He said He can do. Jesus continues to drive this point home in verses 31-47, explaining that there is no life outside of him. You may read the bible and even this devotion, but if you don't believe in the God you are reading about, it is all for nothing. You may be physically attractive, have a successful career, be extremely intelligent, or even a sports champion; but allow me to be clear... There are no true champions in this world except those who have *THE* Champion, Jesus Christ, living in their hearts. So, if you most desperately want to experience real life, listen to God's word and believe in Him... DAILY!

HIS HANDS

Read: John 6:1-15

As we journey into chapter 6, we witness yet another miracle performed by Jesus. 5,000 hungry people, 2 fish, and 5 barley loaves of bread. This in no way sounds like the introduction to a scenario with a positive outcome. But Jesus is in the middle of all of this; and when Jesus is in the middle, the impossible becomes possible. When Jesus is in the middle, the problem becomes a non-issue. When Jesus is in the middle, little becomes much. Jesus takes the little bit of food they have, blesses it and the disciples begin to pass it out. Not only did everyone get full—they had leftovers! This is a reminder to us that in His hands, possibilities are endless. Whatever you need God to bless, touch, stretch or multiply for you; trust Him enough to put it in His hands and leave it there…DAILY!

WATER WALKER

Read: John 6:16-21

◆ ◆ ◆

It is common for God to place choice blessings right outside the borders of our comfort zones, and compel us to come get them. Comfort zones are invisible barriers that cause us to feel safe and cozy. They develop as a result of us doing something in a repetitive fashion over a course of time so much, that they become a part of how we operate. Throughout this passage we see the disciples in a *comfortable* boat on the *uncomfortable* stormy sea, and Jesus comes to them walking on the water! We must not miss the blessing of being reminded that the things which trouble us are already under His feet. Sometimes what we see will scare the heck out of us—but we must trust His voice even when what we see is overwhelming. Jesus spoke to the disciples in the middle of the storm, and He will do the same for us in the midst of ours, if we keep our gaze on Him. Let's make the courageous choice to move from our comfort zone to the exciting faith zone...DAILY!

WORTH IT

Read: John 6:22-71

◆ ◆ ◆

Throughout this passage, Jesus is teaching in the synagogue. He shares some challenging truths that really cause those listening to do some soul searching about whether they truly believe, and how committed they are to following Him. The scripture says, "Therefore, when many of His disciples heard this, they said, 'This teaching is hard, who can accept it?' " (John 6:60). Jesus then goes on to acknowledge that He knows many in the crowd still don't believe: "From that moment many of His disciples turned back and no longer accompanied Him. Therefore Jesus said to the Twelve, 'You don't want to go away too, do you?' " (John 6:66-67). Simple geography says in order to come towards one thing, we must come away from something else; and this is true for us as believers in Jesus also. In order for us to follow Jesus totally, we must unfollow some other people and things in our lives that no longer fit with our new transformed life in Christ. The things we have to release in order to take Christ by the hand aren't always easy to let go of, but what we gain in Jesus is worth it. The Twelve true disciples knew this, and remained faithful. So shall we. Change is difficult, but His ways are right, and His path is the only true path that leads to eternal life. A closer relationship with Jesus is always worth the sacrifice, so may we choose Christ over any other thing in our lives...DAILY!

World hates Jesus because he stands for Good! not evil

IDENTITY

Read: John 7:1-9

◆ ◆ ◆

Knowing who we are, and what we were born to do are extremely important in life. We live in a world of people who are constantly in an identity crisis; searching for meaning, significance, and purpose in things that can never satisfy. When we discover who and more importantly Whose we are, life truly becomes exciting and purpose-filled. One challenge that often remains after discovering our purpose however, is getting others to believe. Nothing is often more discouraging than when those who we care for the most, and are closest to our hearts, don't believe in us. Verse 5 shows us that even in this, our Savior can relate. It says, "For not even His brothers believed in Him" (John 7:5). Don't focus on who isn't with you—focus today on who *is* with you, who *does* support you, and those who *do* believe in all God has blessed you to become. Jesus didn't allow his brothers' disbelief to stop Him from walking in his purpose and we shouldn't either. Let's commit to trust in what God says about us, and lean into His plan for our lives...DAILY!

COVERED

Read: John 7:10-53

◆ ◆ ◆

Throughout these verses, we see trouble brewing as the crowds take sides regarding who Jesus is, and what should be done about Him. Multiple times we've seen people doubting His deity while attempting to seize and even kill Him. Despite their efforts, verses 30 and 44 tell us that they couldn't even lay a hand on Him. We must approach everyday knowing that while people may oppose and wish ill upon us, at the end of the day people are still just people, and God is still God. Jesus knew that His Father had Him covered—so He didn't shrink back, He didn't allow haters to silence Him, or even the threat of death to keep Him from walking in truth. May we follow Christ's example boldly, as we approach the trials, tribulations, and turbulence of life...DAILY!

FORGIVEN

Read: John 8:1-11

◆ ◆ ◆

Chapter 8 begins with Jesus in the temple complex, and a woman caught in the middle of a sinful act is brought to Him. The scribes and Pharisees ask Him what should be done to her as a test. Jesus responds saying, "…the one without sin among you should be the first to throw a stone at her" (John 8:7), and eventually they all left. All of us, like this woman, have sinned in some way before, and fallen short of God's standard by committing an immoral or unlawful act. When Adam and Eve sinned in the garden, sin entered the world. Consequently, sin has been passed down to all of us, which means none of us has the moral capacity to please God in and of ourselves. We can't please God independent of God. We all desperately need His grace and mercy in order to walk in a way pleasing to Him. I'm here to say, as followers of Jesus Christ (and I've had and will have moments like this) even on our best day, sometimes we drift off into sin. We do something we shouldn't and start kicking ourselves—but we must remain patient. We haven't arrived yet…God is just starting a work in us. He won't be done with us until we behold Him face to face. That does not give us a license to sin, but we can walk in the grace of Jesus Christ, knowing we are forgiven…DAILY!

ANYONE

Read: John 8:12-29

◆ ◆ ◆

In this passage, Jesus continues to teach us about who He is and what He has come to Earth to do. Verse 12 stands out as a powerful message for us. It says, "Then Jesus spoke to them again: 'I am the light of the world. Anyone who follows Me will never walk in darkness but will have the light of life'" (John 8:12). Jesus doesn't say He is the light of one region or area, instead He says He is the light of the entire world. Similarly, Jesus doesn't limit his light to a specific race, gender, or class of people...He says ANYONE who follows Him will have His light. At times we feel that because of how we look, where we are from, or what we don't have, we are somehow disqualified from the light of Jesus. That simply isn't true. His light is available to anyone who believes in Him, believes that He is God's only Son, and follows Him. Jesus loves us all, and we should also show love to all...DAILY!

.

The Word → Truth
Truth → set you free

FREE

Read: John 8:30-59

◆ ◆ ◆

As Jesus is speaking to the disciples, we witness a liberating promise. He says, "...If you continue in My word, you really are My disciples. You will know the truth, and the truth will set you free" (John 8:31-32). He goes on to explain what we will be free from: "...I assure you: Everyone who commits sin is a slave of sin. A slave does not remain in the household forever, but a son does remain forever. Therefore, if the Son sets you free, you really will be free" (John 8:34-36). You and I have been made free because the Son of God, Jesus Christ, rescued us. The idea of being rescued means we were in danger. If we're not in Christ we are in *danger*. If someone were to die today outside of Christ, they would spend eternity separated from God. The great tragedy is not being in danger; the tragedy is being in danger and not realizing it. There are so many people who don't know Jesus, who don't even think they need to be rescued, and that's a tragedy. Jesus wants us free, not in bondage. Jesus wants us to be sons, not slaves. Jesus wants us in the light, not darkness. It is the responsibility of those of us who have been set free to go back and tell anyone who will listen, that Jesus Christ is the truth that sets all men free...DAILY!

BIG PICTURE

Read: John 9:1-18

◆ ◆ ◆

We are immediately introduced to this man who has been blind from birth at the opening of chapter 9. In verse 2 the disciples are trying to find out whose fault it is that this man has to deal with this condition. Jesus powerfully responds by saying, "Neither this man nor his parents sinned... This came about so that God's works might be displayed in him" (John 9:3). What this tells us is, every form of adversity or conflict we face is not always because we did something wrong necessarily. Jesus tells us that God allows us to get into certain situations because He wants to show off His strength in our lives. You and I were chosen to face certain challenges, and if we keep the faith, we are going to have the opportunity to see God do something extraordinary in our lives. It gets even deeper in verses 6 and 15 as we see Jesus spit on the ground, make mud in His hands, and then spread the mud into the blind man's eyes in order to heal him. This extends another powerful lesson to us—to not get caught up in the process, but to instead look towards the big picture. Jesus' plan to heal the blind man involved the man having to get muddy first, and we also have to get muddy sometimes before we experience a breakthrough. God's plan may involve us going to some muddy places or dealing with some muddy people or some muddy circumstances... but if we trust and obey Christ through the muddy moments, we will see the miraculous happen. We must stop looking around for something or someone to blame, and start looking up to God whose plan is perfect and is our strength...DAILY!

STILL ME

Read: John 9:19-41

◆ ◆ ◆

Jesus performed such a miraculous work in this man's life that nobody could believe it. All throughout the rest of the chapter we hear the opinions and questions of everyone from neighbors, to the Pharisees—even his parents were questioned. God is doing a similar transformation in us as well. The more He opens our eyes and the further we walk with Him, the less we will be like our old selves. People will doubt, wonder, and debate whether it's still the same us or if its a trick…but like the blind man kept telling everyone, we also get to tell others, "it's still me!" The difference is we were once blind, but because of Jesus and the light found in the life of Christ, now we see! Now, pay attention to the part where they eventually throw the man out in frustration. We will also be thrown out of certain circles because of our faith. That is okay. This *former* blind man was thrown out in verse 34, but in verse 35 he was face to face again with Jesus. We never lose when we choose a life in Christ above all else…DAILY!

GOOD SHEPHERD

Read: John 10:1-21

Act like Jesus as a leader!
- Jesus

◆ ◆ ◆

Chapter 10 opens with Jesus giving multiple illustrations, explaining the difference between a good and bad shepherd. We can also use these examples to learn the difference between a good and bad leader. In the first two verses, Jesus highlights the importance of the true shepherd entering through the door and not entering any other way. We learn here the importance of a leader having integrity and not cutting corners. Next, Jesus begins to discuss the importance of the shepherd knowing his sheep by name and them knowing his voice. This tells us how important relationship and rapport are for a great leader. It is important that those you lead don't just see you as someone giving out orders, but someone they have a connection and mutual sense of purpose with. Jesus explains in verse 10 that a bad leader steals, kills, and destroys those he leads. Then Jesus, *the greatest leader ever,* contrasts that idea by saying He "...comes that they might have life and have it in abundance" (John10:10). A great leader wants the entire team to win, and understands the importance of unity. Maybe the most powerful measure of leadership comes between verses 11 and 13, when Jesus explains that a good shepherd lays his life down for his sheep, but a bad one abandons his sheep in the face of danger. Is that the type of leader you would want to follow? Of course not. May we all strive to be leaders who put the needs of our people above ourselves, and lead with courage...DAILY!

TRUE SHEEP

Read: John 10:22-30

◆ ◆ ◆

After giving us verse after verse about the makings of a good shepherd, Jesus then gives us keys to the DNA of His sheep. He says, "But you do not believe because you are not My sheep. My sheep hear My voice, I know them, and they follow Me. I give them eternal life, and they will never perish- ever! No one will snatch them out of My hand" (John 10:26-28). The first thing we learn here about a true follower of Jesus is that they are believers. We must remain unshakable in our faith in Christ, our Good Shepherd. Next, we must remain obedient to the voice of our Shepherd. Jesus then says "I know them", again highlighting an actual relationship. Obviously, if we are truly His sheep we must follow Him. How do we follow Him? By trusting that we are safe in His hands, listening to and obeying His voice, and seeking to grow deeper in our relationship with Him...DAILY!

ACTION

Read: John 10:31-42

◆ ◆ ◆

By the end of this chapter the Jews have picked up rocks and are ready to stone Jesus. Then He says something that is important for us to reflect on: "If I am not doing My Father's works, don't believe Me. But if I am doing them and you don't believe Me, believe the works. This way you will know and understand that the Father is in Me and I in the Father" (John 10:37-38). Jesus basically says, even if you don't believe in Me, you can't deny the work I am doing! Jesus invites these people who are ready to kill Him, to judge Him based solely on His actions, if they must. We know we have repented of our sin, prayed and asked Christ into our heart, and even been reading the bible...but what does the way we live say about who we serve? Does the way we treat people and approach life represent our Savior well? What if people ignored what we have been saying with our mouths and solely judged us based on how we behave? Not just in good times, when everything is going well...but in times of pressure and adversity. Ideas are worthless, intentions have no power, and plans are nothing unless they are followed with action. We must make sure that as followers of Jesus, we are more than just lip service, we must walk out what we confess to believe...DAILY!

His perfect plan!

NO MISTAKES

Read: John 11:1-37

◆ ◆ ◆

Chapter 11 is dominated by this compelling account of Jesus and his friend Lazarus, who dies and four days later, Jesus raises from the dead! Jesus performs yet another sign that demonstrates He is sent from God and truly the Messiah. One interesting detail in this account is that many people thought Jesus had made a mistake by not arriving in time before Lazarus dies. Upon Jesus' arrival Martha rushes to meet Him and says, "Lord, if You had been here my brother wouldn't have died" (John 11:21). A short time later, Mary also goes to Jesus and says the exact same thing. Finally, as they are watching this scenario unfold, some of the Jews respond in a similar way saying,   "...Couldn't He who opened the blind man's eyes also have kept this man from dying?" (John 11:37). They all assumed that Jesus made a mistake by not healing him before he died. Let this be a lesson to us now and forever...Jesus doesn't make any mistakes. God's plan for Lazarus was perfect, and His plans for you and I are perfect as well. These are the times when faith comes into play most. When we can't trust what we see, we must trust what God says. Look again at what Jesus told Martha: "Your brother will rise again" (John 11:23). Remember that when it comes to our Savior and our walk with Him in this life, it will all work out in the end. If it's not worked out, it's not the end. Jesus makes no mistakes. We are not forgotten, we are not forsaken, God can and will come through for us. So while we wait for Jesus to show up in these difficult circumstances in and around our lives, may we remember His plan is perfect, and we are wise to trust Him...DAILY!

Trust God's Timing

NEVER TOO LATE

Read: John 11:38-57

◆ ◆ ◆

Another lesson we learn from this chapter is that when Jesus is involved it is never too late. Lazarus is dead and in a tomb when Jesus tells the people to remove the stone. Martha responds by telling Jesus, "...Lord, he's already decaying, its been four days" (John 11:39). Martha (and undoubtedly everyone else present) thought it was too late, but Jesus calls him by name saying, "Lazarus, come out!"(John 11:43), and he did! What things in our lives have we put in a tomb? What relationships? Dreams? Possibilities? Have we made the same mistake that Martha did, by trusting what we see over what God has said? We must remember that one word from Jesus can change everything. So no matter how many days, weeks, months, or even years it has been—it is never too late for Jesus to speak life into something. So let's remove the stone we have placed over our dead situations and trust God to awaken them again. May we all trust God's timing...DAILY!

HATERS

Read: John 12:1-11

◆ ◆ ◆

People often hate what they don't understand. This is demonstrated as we begin chapter 12, where we read around verse 9 that the Jews have decided they also want to kill Lazarus, because of what Jesus has done in his life. This will be true for many of us as well. Just because people don't understand what God has done in our lives, or why He chose to do something great for us right now instead of them, many people will oppose us. Some will hate us because God is shining His light in and through us. Some will even wish harm upon us. They may not try to literally kill us (in some countries they will), but they may try desperately to assassinate our character, persecute us, turn others against us, or even desire to see us ruin our witness. We can't focus on haters, we must focus on trusting God deeply, and loving people authentically. Love always wins in the end. So let them hate, while we continue to love them with the love of Christ...DAILY!

STAY LOW

Read: John 12:12-19

◆ ◆ ◆

One of the first things American football coaches teach linemen is the importance of leverage. One phrase often used is "the low man always wins", and if you ever get a chance to compete or watch the battles between offensive and defensive linemen, you will see this statement often rings true. This truth can be universally embraced as a blueprint for life, and as a reminder to stay humble. Jesus, the great King of Kings that He is, demonstrates this in these verses we just read. As He is entering Jerusalem, this crowd of people is trying to make a big deal about Him. Instead of basking in all of the pageantry, Jesus quickly finds and jumps on a donkey, instantly changing the picture they see. The truth is, if He wanted that glory, He could have chosen to ride in on a horse, demonstrating a strong, traditional picture of a King returning from war. Instead, by riding in on a donkey Jesus demonstrates a picture of peace and humility. May we all remember to not take the glory for ourselves, but instead always remain humble, pointing people back to our King, Jesus. Let's stay low...DAILY!

LIFTED

Read: John 12:20-50

◆ ◆ ◆

Throughout these verses, many things take place. Jesus predicts His crucifixion in verses 20-36, fulfills Isaiah's prophecies in 37-43, and finally we see a summary of His mission in verses 44 through 50. Let's focus specifically on the moment when Jesus says, "As for Me, if I am lifted up from the earth I will draw all people to Myself" (John 12:32). Jesus is giving us a sneak peek into the formula that will be necessary for you and I to have a shot at eternal life. Jesus knew that He came to Earth to pay a price that only He was qualified to pay. Because of Jesus being lifted up on that old rugged cross, we also have the opportunity to be raised with Him. Raised from our sin, raised from darkness, raised from our past, and raised from condemnation. Jesus was preparing to pay the ultimate price, and He knew it. The price we now must pay as believers follows the same formula Jesus revealed earlier. We must continue to lift Jesus up so that all people can be drawn to Him. Let's lift Him up in the way we walk, talk, live, give, serve, and love...DAILY!

SERVANT LEADER

Read: John 13:1-20

◆ ◆ ◆

In possibly the most powerful picture of true leadership, we witness Jesus wash the feet of His disciples and teach them what it really means. Jesus originated true servant leadership, and in no greater place than John chapter 13 do we see this. Jesus humbles Himself and shows His disciples how He wants them to serve each other, even after He has departed. Many people mistake leadership for being the loudest or the shiniest or the meanest, but Jesus shows us that true strength is displayed in being a servant to those you lead. May we all serve like Jesus served...DAILY!

UNCONDITIONAL

Read: John 13:21-30

◆ ◆ ◆

Jesus is washing feet, teaching, and breaking bread right now. However, we later discover that Jesus knows a man at this table will betray Him, and another will deny Him. Wait a minute— He knows they are going to turn their backs on Him, but He is serving and loving on them anyway? Wow. This is the same Jesus that lives in our hearts now. That means we have the capacity to show uncompromising character and integrity as well. If we want to know whether we're loving people, we must ask: How do we handle the people that get on our last nerve? How do we interact with people who can't do anything for us? How do we treat people who, if we were on fire and they had a glass of water, wouldn't pour it on us, but would instead drink it slowly? Jesus didn't allow the actions of others to dictate how He approached life and people. May we authentically reek of Jesus! This doesn't mean we have to be perfect, but even in our imperfections may we ask for forgiveness, and let people know that what we've said and done were not in line with the truth of the gospel. May we remain unwavering in our loving treatment of people...DAILY!

PROOF

Read: John 13:31-38

◆ ◆ ◆

As the final supper with His disciples continues, Jesus issues a new command: "…Love one another. Just as I have loved you, you must also love one another. By this all people will know that you are My disciples, if you have love for one another" (John 13:34-35). Jesus says that our identifying marker as His disciples is not our church attendance, how much money we have, or how many bible verses we know. Instead, Jesus says if we love each other, all people will know that we are His. Faith gives us access to the gospel, but love is what attests to others that the gospel is inside of us. The Greek word for love is "agape," which means a sacrificial love that seeks the best in the object of such love. You know you love someone when you lay down your life for them. May we honor the example of Christ by loving without limits…DAILY!

THE PATH

Read: John 14:1-11

◆ ◆ ◆

Earth is not our home; we are just passing through this life. Everyone lives forever somewhere. In the beginning of this chapter, Jesus makes a powerful promise to His disciples, and to us as believers today. He says, "If I go away and prepare a place for you, I will come back and receive you to Myself, so that where I am you may be also" (John 14:3). Our focus should always remain eternal and fixed on being with Christ. Jesus gives us directions to that place when He goes on to say, "...I am the way, the truth, and the life. No one comes to the Father except through Me" (John 14:6). Jesus leaves no room for interpretation —He is clear that He is the only path to true salvation. He didn't say that He is "a" way, truth, and life....Jesus says He is *THE* way, truth, and life. We live in a world where many believe truth is relative, but clearly Jesus didn't teach that. May we all remain on the path created by Jesus Christ, the Son of God...DAILY!

NEVER ALONE

Read: John 14:12-26

◆ ◆ ◆

In this passage, Jesus continues to reveal monumental truths to His disciples. He says, "If you ask anything in My name I will do it" (John 14:14). A few verses later,   He declares, "I will not leave you as orphans, I am coming to you"(John 14:18). Finally He promises, "If anyone loves Me, he will keep My word. My Father will love him, and We will come to him and make Our home with him" (John 14:23). Jesus packs this section of the chapter with verse after verse reaffirming that we are never alone. Now that we have invited Him to live in our hearts, He is with us wherever we may go. Jesus is a father to the fatherless, a mother to those who may be motherless, even a friend to those of us who may be currently friendless. Our true purpose and significance is revealed inside of a relationship with Jesus. May we feel the warmth, comfort, and love of Jesus and His Spirit which has taken residence in our hearts...DAILY!

IRREPLACEABLE

Read: John 14:27-31

◆ ◆ ◆

As our reading begins, Jesus says, "Peace I leave with you. My peace I give to you. I do not give it to you as the world gives. Your heart must not be troubled or fearful" (John 14:27). Jesus refers to His peace He gives us as a gift, and a precious gift it is. It is a gift we must take hold of and never let go; a gift that we must guard emphatically. There are people who have endless riches, and still don't have peace. Some have global notoriety and popularity, but have no peace. Jesus is the Prince of Peace, and He tells us in this verse, not that He is giving us *some* peace... No, Jesus says "MY PEACE I give to you". There is one stipulation though, Jesus instructs us to not allow our hearts to be troubled or fearful. May we all walk in the peace of Jesus Christ...DAILY!

FRUIT

Read: John 15:1-15

◆ ◆ ◆

Chapter 15 opens with Jesus telling us that He is the vine, and God the Father is the vineyard keeper. He then proceeds to teach us the importance of fruit in our lives. The way we know that we're saved is not because we repeated a prayer alone, not because mom and dad are, and not because we go to bible study or chapel. Jesus says the way we know we are saved is fruit! It's a changed and changing lifestyle that can only be blamed on the power of God. If our testimony is we accepted Christ, but we're the same person we were 10 years ago… How can these both be true? No, the gospel changes people! It changed a persecutor named Paul, it changed a denier named Peter, and it changed a murderer named Moses. It changes us all! The Gospel is the news that Jesus Christ, the Righteous One, died for our sins and rose again, eternally triumphant over all His enemies. As a result, there is now no condemnation for those who believe, but only everlasting joy. Jesus didn't come into our hearts to merely rearrange the furniture…He wants to blow the house up! May the fruit of our lives produce faith, love, and hope…DAILY!

HAND-PICKED

Read: John 15:16-27

Despite our flaws, insecurities, shortcomings, past, and humanity, Jesus declares, "You did not choose Me, but I chose you…" (John 15:16). Yes, Jesus chose us. He knew all the mistakes we would make, and how desperately we would need Him to just make it one day in this Christian walk, and chose us anyway. He knows the real us, not the representative that we send out when we are trying to impress others and put our best foot forward. Knowing all He knows, He still thought we were worth dying for, to give us an opportunity to have everlasting life. We were hand-picked to glorify God and approach every area of our lives with the mind of Christ. Hand-picked, to overcome the obstacles He allows us to face, and hand-picked, to slay the giants we are often confronted with. May we always remember we have been chosen by a God who makes no mistakes…DAILY!

REFEREE

Read: John 16:1-15

◆ ◆ ◆

In every sport there are two teams that compete against each other for a prize. These competitions are always officiated by one or more people tasked with providing order, ensuring safety, and maintaining fairness during the game. This team of officials has the responsibility to make sure each competitor obeys the rules of the game, and blows the whistle if someone breaks the rules. These referees make sure the game flows appropriately. Throughout this passage, Jesus begins to teach about the Holy Spirit, and Its function in our lives as believers. The Holy Spirit is in many ways our referee in life. Jesus refers to the Holy Spirit as a Counselor, and says that "...He will convict the world about sin, righteousness, and judgement" (John 16:8). Conviction in its simplest form means the Holy Spirit letting us know when we need a little more or a little less of something. Jesus goes on to call it the Spirit of Truth and says, "...He will guide [us] in all truth..." (John 16:13). God has given us, as followers of Jesus, the precious gift of this Counselor, assigned to lead and guide us along this journey.

We must be obedient to the leading of God's Holy Spirit as it maintains order and flow in our walk with Christ, ensuring that we pursue a path pleasing to Him. May we trust the instruction, conviction, truth, voice, and counsel of the Holy Spirit...DAILY!

PAIN TO POWER

Read: John 16:16-33

◆ ◆ ◆

There is a very popular phrase in sports that says "no pain, no gain". This phrase is purposed to communicate how important it is to push through grueling exercise and training in order to see your desired results, and become a better and more effective competitor. Jesus teaches a similar concept in this particular passage by telling His disciples how soon their sorrow will be turned into joy. There are certain things in life we can't go around, over, or underneath…some things we must go right through. However, these are the tests and trials of life that truly make us better people. If we reflect over our lives, I am sure we all can see how the things that caused us the most pain taught us the biggest lessons; enhancing our appreciation for life. Jesus shares these encouraging words with His disciples: "I have told you these things so that in Me you may have peace. You will have suffering in this world. Be courageous! I have conquered the world" (John 16:33). Jesus is being very clear with us here—adversity is coming. However, he quickly reminds us that He has already won it all on our behalf.Tough times do not last, tough people do. It is our responsibility to remain forward focused in all that we go through in life, knowing that Jesus will turn our weeping into rejoicing, sorrow into joy, and pain into power. May we lean into life, and not allow anyone or anything to rob us of our joy…DAILY!

PURPOSE

Read: John 17:1-5

◆ ◆ ◆

This chapter begins with a very passionate prayer from Jesus, as He talks to His heavenly Father. Jesus professes to God, "I have glorified You on the earth by completing the work You gave Me to do" (John 17:4). Jesus sets the standard for all believers, regarding what we should aspire to be able to declare to God someday as well. Are we glorifying God with our lives on Earth? How do we glorify Him? We glorify God on Earth just like Jesus did, by "completing the work" God has given us individually, and collectively, as is required for all who believe. We must focus on God's purpose for our lives, and ensure we are doing that work well. Jesus knew that He came to earth to serve a very specific purpose, and today we must also be aware that God has a plan for our lives too. If we don't yet know what that purpose is, we should do as Jesus instructs us chapter after chapter in the book of John, and ask in His name. We should be praying day and night, seeking and asking, and listening to the leading of the Holy Spirit until we discover what God has called us to do. After we discover what were born to do, it is imperative that we make that work, that calling, and that duty our obsession until completion. Not for our glory, but all for His. May we fulfill our God ordained purpose by completing the work God has given us to do...DAILY!

TEAM

Read: John 17:6-19

From the very first chapter in the book of John, we saw how Jesus began to assemble a team. His disciples were not a band of perfect men, but they were a group of guys working and walking together to accomplish a specific goal. Even the disciple that is to betray Jesus (Judas) has a purpose to serve in order to fulfill God's plan. Throughout this passage, Jesus is praying to God for His disciples...for His team. How interesting is it that Jesus prays for himself for just five verses, but is praying for His disciples for fourteen? This shows us yet another glimpse into the heart of the Good Shepherd. He is about to be sacrificed for the sins of the world, but Jesus is more concerned about His team than Himself. We all need a team, a tribe, a support system, a family. There is no such thing as a lone ranger Christian. After we encounter Jesus Christ, He wants us to encounter His people. We need to be connected to other believers and experience fellowship, accountability, and community. We need someone praying for us, encouraging us, and battling with us—and we need to provide the same to others. Jesus had this, and we need it as well. May we pray for our team, lift up our tribe, and walk courageously with our brothers and sisters in Christ...DAILY!

UNITY

Read: John 17:20-26

◆ ◆ ◆

In our final seven verses of this chapter, Jesus actually prays for us. Yes, you and I. More than anything else, Jesus prays literally over and over that we as believers will become one in Him. Jesus explains that the key to the world believing in Christ is us as believers being "…made completely one…" (John 17:23). If we want to please God and see the world impacted most powerfully for Jesus Christ, we will have to accomplish that as one. Not just *together*, but literally as one. This means we must find a way to eliminate all the division that currently exists among believers around our world. We must not allow denomination, race, pride, or any of those other dividers to separate us any longer. It is time for the people of God to stand up as one, so that the world may believe in Jesus Christ. May we tear down walls that divide, and build bridges…DAILY!

OWN IT

Read: John 18:1-27

◆ ◆ ◆

There is no such thing as high or low integrity...either we have it or we do not. As we read through this portion of chapter 18, we witness such an intriguing contrast. On one hand we have Peter, who is repeatedly questioned about his affiliation with Jesus, and who in the face of adversity, denies Him. *Three* different times, asked by *three* different people, Peter denies being a disciple of Jesus Christ. This same man, who in verse 10 cut a man's ear off seemingly to defend Jesus, now denies even being a follower. Peter was one type of man in the presence of Jesus, and another man when the pressure was on. This is not godly character. On the contrary, we see this group of men approaching the garden that Jesus and His disciples are in, carrying lanterns, torches and weapons. Does Jesus retreat? Lie about His identity? Blame someone else? Make excuses? The answer is no. Our courageous Savior, and ultimate model for authentic manhood, approaches them head on, and is actually the one who initiates communication with those He already knows have come to harm Him. This passage tell us that "...Jesus, knowing everything that was about to happen to Him, went out and said to them, 'Who is it you are looking for?' 'Jesus the Nazarene,' they answered. 'I am He', Jesus told them..." (John 18:4-5). With no hesitation, without fear or excuse, Jesus owns the moment. He embraced the challenge ahead, and so must we. We must commit to resist the urge to cut corners or compromise, despite what consequence that may mean for us. May we do what is right, because it is right...DAILY!

PASSION

Read: John 18:28-40

◆ ◆ ◆

For the rest of this chapter, we witness Jesus being captured and then taken to Pilate, where the Jews want Him to be sentenced to death. Jesus is in the headquarters with the man in position to judge whether He will be put to death or not, and they are having a conversation. Towards the end of their dialogue, Jesus says, "...I was born for this, and I have come into the world for this: to testify to the truth..." (John 18:37). Jesus speaks to His passion, His *Why*, as He confidently tells this man that He knows what He was on Earth to do. Passion is more important than a plan. Passion provides fuel. Passion creates fire! We must walk in our passion—living out loud, courageously, and intentionally. Most people in the world waste their life chasing things that are empty. We as followers of Jesus Christ have the opportunity to live our lives for something much bigger than ourselves. We must each make a crucial decision: Will I live to serve self, or live to experience the liberating winds of freedom that Christ desires for us? Moment by moment, decision by decision, we will either choose freedom or bondage. A life centered on Jesus is a life of fullness. There is meaning, substance and satisfaction when Christ alone is our passion for living. May we passionately live out what we were born to do...DAILY!

CHOICES

Read: John 19:1-16

◆ ◆ ◆

Our Savior has done nothing wrong, yet chapter 19 opens with Him being beaten, mocked, and slapped. Pilate is still trying to decide what to do with Jesus, and for fifteen verses goes back and forth with the Jews about what should happen to Him. Pilate admits repeatedly, that he finds no fault in Jesus and has no grounds to kill Him, but the Jews refuse to be denied. After immense pressure, we see Pilate finally fold when the verse says, "so then, because of them, he handed Him over to be crucified" (John 19:16). Pilate allows the voices and influence of others to dictate what he chooses to do with Jesus. We must not make this same mistake. We must not allow people to keep us from doing the right things. We must not allow the opinions of others to cause us to ignore our own heart and conscience. God calls us to serve others, but it is not our job to be in the people pleasing business. Truth is, the "people" will never be pleased. What is God speaking to you? What has Jesus placed in your heart? What is the Holy Spirit directing you to accomplish? May we stay true to our King, and ignore the crowd… DAILY!

NO MATTER WHAT

Read: John 19:17-27

◆ ◆ ◆

Here we see Jesus having to carry His own cross, to be crucified between two thieves. The Savior of the world is being put to death, and guess who is right there by His side? Our passage says that, "standing by the cross of Jesus was His mother, His mother's sister, Mary the wife of Clopas, and Mary Magdalene" (John 19:25). Her innocent son is being executed, and Jesus' mother is still right there by His side. There is nothing like a mother's love. Mothers are there for us through thick and thin, they are our first friend, our first teacher, and our first introduction to love and affection. We would all be a mess if it wasn't for our mother's precious love. Even if it's not our mother—whoever has stuck with us through our toughest and lowest moments, has rooted for us to be our best, and helped us become who we are today—we owe them. We owe them honor, we owe them gratitude, we owe them thanks, and we owe them appreciation. We should contact those special people who are on our side and in our corner unconditionally, and let them know how much they mean to us. Let's commit to also being in someone else's corner no matter what, and supporting them in prayer, with encouraging words, and acts of love. May we be a source of strength and support to others...DAILY!

FINISHER

Read: John 19:28-42

◆ ◆ ◆

As we complete chapter 19, we see Jesus is crucified, and gives His life for the sins of the world. In the ultimate act of sacrifice, our Savior lays His life down for His sheep. Before Jesus gives up His life, He declares, "...it is finished..." (John 19:30). Our King, our Savior, our Champion is a finisher. Now, let's be clear... Jesus said, "it is finished" not "I am finished," because we know Jesus was just getting started! We as believers also have the opportunity to represent Christ by likewise being finishers. Finishers are the game changers on a team, finishers are the difference makers on a staff, finishers are the rock of communities. There is something honorable about men and women who finish what they start. Jesus gave everything at the finish, and we also have a responsibility to persevere to the end. May we live full and die empty because we gave life all we had. Let us all establish ourselves as finishers for the glory of God...DAILY!

RAISED

Read: John 20:1-18

◆ ◆ ◆

The stone has been removed. The tomb is empty. Jesus has been raised from the dead! This is the great news of the Gospel of Jesus Christ. Throughout this passage we see testimony of Jesus proving once and for all, He is the Messiah. Jesus came to Earth and lived a perfect life, a life you and I couldn't live. Then He dies the death that we deserve to die. We are the ones who sinned, not Him. We are the ones who broke God's law, but in His great love for us, God sends His Son to die in our place, and for our sins. The biggest and most significant part happens next… God raises Jesus from the dead! This means that Jesus is who He said He is, and He can do what He said He can do! Because Jesus was raised from the dead, we have been raised from the guilt and shame of sin. Because Jesus was raised from the dead, we can be raised from the issues, negativities, and problems of this world that try to pin us down and trap us. May we continue to rise with Jesus…DAILY!

DELIVER

Read: John 20:19-31

◆ ◆ ◆

Jesus reveals Himself to His mother, then to His disciples. He begins to commission and empower them to go out and fulfill their purpose. As we read through the rest of chapter 20, we see Jesus meeting people right where they are, figuratively and literally. Both times that the disciples were gathered (verses 19 & 26), the bible says that the doors were locked, but Jesus showed up anyway. Jesus knows exactly where we are, and He is able and willing to meet us there. Jesus also knows our level of faith. Thomas needed to put his finger through the hole in Jesus' hands and his hand through the hole in Jesus' side—and Jesus accommodates him. Listen, Jesus knows where we are, and whatever we are wrestling with, He wants to meet us there. We must however, invite Him in so that He can help us. What areas of your life do you need Jesus to deliver? What do you need from the Savior? He can and will meet us right where we are, but will never leave us the same way. His transforming, mighty, healing hand is available to us all, but we must reach out and touch it. May we know that God will deliver what we need, when we need it...DAILY!

MORE

Read: John 21:1-14

◆ ◆ ◆

As chapter 21 begins, Peter is with many other disciples. He then abruptly decides he is going to go fishing. The others also decide to go and jump in the boat with him. Collectively, they fish all night and catch absolutely nothing. Many of us have often found ourselves in similar situations. Maybe it wasn't in a boat, but we can relate to making decisions on our own—going out, working all day and all night in our own strength, and getting absolutely nowhere. These men had worked in their own strength and wisdom with nothing to show for it. Then when day finally broke through, Jesus stood on the shore and said, "Men... you don't have any fish, do you? 'No', they answered" (John 21:5). Two things happen in those verses that are classically true of Jesus. First, we learn that when we are down to nothing, God is often up to something. Jesus appears after giving them plenty of time to do things their own way, and coming up empty. Secondly, have you noticed throughout scripture how often Jesus asks questions He already knows the answers to? Jesus asks about their fish count, and the men admit they have caught nothing. God often asks questions He already knows the answers to so that He can give us these moments of clarity—to be real with ourselves and with Him. As the next nine verses unfold, we see Jesus giving them instruction on fishing His way, and they receive unthinkable results. The passage says, "...they were unable to haul it in because of the large number of fish" (John 21:6). Doing things all night their way gets them nothing; when they do things as Christ instructs just once, they catch more fish than they can handle. This is a lesson for us all: We will always gain more following Christ's instructions than doing things our own way. May we remember that God can do more for us in thirty seconds, than we could do for ourselves in thirty years. Let's commit to doing life His way...DAILY!

REDEEMED

Read: John 21:15-23

◆ ◆ ◆

As Jesus is speaking to Peter, we witness this redemptive moment between them. Now we all know Peter had just in chapter 18 denied Jesus three different times, and is seeing the risen Savior for the third time now. I'm sure Peter's denial was weighing heavy on his mind and heart. Jesus intriguingly asks Peter the same question three times: "Do you love Me?" Peter's answer is always the same: "You know that I love You". Jesus is again showing us as believers how deep, long, and wide His love is for us. Jesus doesn't just end His relationship with Peter because of what he has done—Jesus gives Peter another chance to be redeemed. The love and grace of Jesus is available to us all. So no matter what we have done, no matter what we have become; we can go back to Jesus and be renewed if we are willing to turn back to Him, repent, and be restored. Jesus reached us all when we were unreachable, loved us when we were unloveable, and forgave us when we did the unforgivable. May we abandon our way of doing things, and commit to His path and plan for our lives...DAILY!

HOPE

Read: John 21:24-25

◆ ◆ ◆

The book of John ends with this: "And there are also many other things that Jesus did, which, if they were written one by one, I suppose not even the world itself could contain the books that would be written" (John 21:25). This tells us that the miraculous life, death, and resurrection we just read about is just the tip of the iceberg in comparison to the width and depth of all Jesus is and shall be. This is where the hope of believers is rooted. In Jesus. It is all about Him. It always has been, and always will be about Him—Jesus, our Redeemer and our Hope. Hope is the foundational quality of all change. Hope is the activator that's necessary in all of our lives. When Hope enters the picture, action is what organically follows. Hope in Jesus should make you and I want to do something! Jesus desires for us to take action and live a life that makes Him proud to be our God. May we allow Jesus to write His story on the tablet of our hearts and lives, so all those we encounter and influence can bear witness and be inspired. Let's commit to showing the world that Jesus is the Hope our world needs...DAILY!

THE END

THE END

ABOUT THE AUTHOR

C.l. "Shep" Shepherd

One of 15 siblings, growing up Shep endured challenges that most would only encounter through the fictional medium of television. As a result, his transparent, and impactful story has captivated thousands, subsequently leading people to transformed lives in droves.

As a former student-athlete, Shep was blessed to participate on every level of competition. He experienced massive success on the football field, but maintains that his proudest accomplishment was earned in the classroom by being the first in his family to graduate from college. Upon graduation, he was then blessed to train in the National Football League. It was after completing his football career that Shep was propelled into his life's work of delivering hope through his speaking to audiences around the world.

Today as an Author, Keynote Speaker, and Character Coach... his passion, dedication, and commitment to growth has fueled his ascension to remarkable heights. His devotion to seeing lives changed is undeniable as he connects deeply with people from all walks of life.

In 2010 he founded Keep The Change Inc, his non-profit organization devoted to empowering pro and college athletes through chaplaincy and mentoring. As CEO of Shep Inspires LLC, he has been unmatched in his ability to deliver real, relevant, and relatable content for over 16 years. His presentations are as relevant as they are timeless. His influence is global. He is one of the leading authorities today on Hope and Transformation. His philosophy is simple: Tough times do not last, Tough people do! He was born in the hood, but he is now reaching the world.

CPSIA information can be obtained
at www.ICGtesting.com
Printed in the USA
LVHW081652120422
716018LV00015B/678

9 780578 863672